Finding Birds in

Introduction

The Canary Islands are located 100km or more from the co[...] makes a massive difference to the avifauna. The first thing t[...] crossing from Africa to become regular breeding birds so a v[...] ..y the relative lack of species. However, as the arrival of birds from Africa is a rare [...] ..., those that **have** made it have remained separated from the rest of the African population and have reached various stages along the route of evolving into separate species. Birds such as Blue Chaffinch, Fuerteventura Chat, Bolle's Pigeon and White-tailed Laurel Pigeon have long been recognised as distinct species, endemic to the Canaries, while other unique species such as Plain Swift, Canary and Berthelot's Pipit are restricted to these islands plus Madeira and/or the Azores. More recently though, an increasing number of Canarian forms have gained species status so Canarian Chiffchaff and Tenerife Goldcrest have been added to the endemics and others such as Tenerife Robin will surely follow suit. A further complication is that some forms have not just been isolated from the African forms, they've also been separated from the populations on the other islands too! Hence the Dutch Birding Association already recognise 4 species of Blue Tit on the Canaries and there's a chance that two forms of Goldcrest and 4 types of Chaffinch will later become 'split' as unique species. There are 'new' endemics among the seabirds too, with the newly split 'Baroli's' Shearwater and two forms of Madeiran Storm-petrel breeding around the Canaries. So, even if you've been to the Canaries before, the chances are you'll be wanting to come again to have another look at these 'new' species.

If you do, you'll also have a chance to enjoy some of the most exciting seawatching in the Western Palearctic and the best opportunities in the world for watching desert birds such as Houbara Bustard - if you know where to find them. That's where this book comes in - providing you with exact details of where to find the endemics such as both laurel pigeons (even on Tenerife) and desert birds such as Houbaras. Where other sources describe 'tracks west of Teguise' or 'tracks near La Pared' this book, with its uniquely detailed maps and GPS co-ordinates, gives you infinitely more detail to get you to the best places.

I hope this book helps you to enjoy some of the great birding on offer on these unique islands and that the DVD enables you to study the various races and species in advance of your visit so you are better informed when you arrive.

Dave Gosney

Acknowledgements

In planning my most recent trip to the Canaries, the most helpful sources I used, apart from my original 'Finding Birds' book, were the Birdwatchers Guide to the Canaries by Clarke and Collins, Where to Watch Birds in Tenerife by Garcia del Rey and the video 'Birds of the Macaronesian Islands' by Leo Boon as well as a multitude of trip reports and news from various correspondents including those who have contributed to the free Finding Birds app. Special mention must go to Richard Bonser and Frances Gatens whose contributions were particularly helpful and Brian Small who was kind enough to confirm that I had looked in the right place for Houbaras at La Pared. While I was in the Canaries I also picked up other useful snippets from other birders, most notably Tony Blunden and Graham Hogan. The pelagic trip could not have been so successful if not for the skills, knowledge and expertise of Dani Lopez-Velasco and his team at lanzarotepelagics.com.

Lastly I again have to thank my ever-tolerant partner Liz Hall who this time had to endure two whole days and nights in the Atlantic on a pitching boat in her determination to make our DVD as good as possible.

The Canary Islands

It is helpful to think of the Canaries as two groups of islands. Those in the western group (El Hierro, La Palma, La Gomera, Tenerife and Gran Canaria) are all well-wooded, at least in parts. You need to visit at least one of these if you want to see the birds of Laurel or Pine forests such as Blue Chaffinch, Chaffinch, Tenerife Goldcrest, Tenerife Robin, Canarian Chiffchaff and, of course, the laurel pigeons. The eastern islands (Fuerteventura and Lanzarote) have very limited woodland but are notable for desert birds especially Houbara Bustard, Cream-coloured Courser, Black-bellied Sandgrouse, Egyptian Vulture, Lesser Short-toed Lark and Trumpeter Finch. All the islands have Berthelot's Pipit, Plain Swift, Canary and Blue Tits, though the last three species are scarcer in the eastern isles. Exciting seabirds are possible around any of these islands. The following describes the particular appeal, or lack of it, of each island.

Tenerife has the most complete assemblage of endemic forest birds including Blue Chaffinch (*Fringilla teydea teydea*), Tenerife Robin (*Erithacus (rubecula) superbus*), Tenerife Goldcrest (*Regulus (regulus) teneriffae*), both laurel pigeons, Tenerife Blue Tit (*Cyanistes (teneriffae) teneriffae*) and a Chaffinch (*Fringilla coelebs tintillon*).

Gran Canaria has the same forms of Robin and Chaffinch as Tenerife and the Blue Tit has recently been claimed to be a unique race/species (*C.t. hedwigii*). This is the only other place in the world where Blue Chaffinch occurs (a different race, *F.t. polatzeki*) but this species is hard to find here due to its scarcity and restricted access. Therefore, since the island also has no laurel pigeons or Tenerife Goldcrest it is generally overlooked by birdwatchers and isn't considered further here.

La Gomera has similar species and races to those on Tenerife except that the Robins here are of the same race/species found in Europe. Many birders visit La Gomera on a day trip from Tenerife, partly because the laurel pigeons are easier to see here but also because there's a chance of seabirds such as Bulwer's Petrel and Macaronesian Shearwater (= Little Shearwater of the form *baroli*) from the ferry *en route*.

La Palma is similar to La Gomera except that the laurel pigeons are even more numerous and easy to see and this island has its own distinctive forms of Blue Tit (*C.t. palmae*) and Chaffinch *(F.c. palmae)* which may merit separate species status. The Goldcrest here is of a race more closely related to European Goldcrest (*Regulus regulus*) and has been claimed to be a distinct subspecies *R.r. ellenthalerae*, unique to La Palma and El Hierro.

El Hierro also has its own unique Blue Tits (*C.t. ombriosus*) and Chaffinches (*F.c. ombriosa*) which may be distinct species but White-tailed Laurel Pigeon is widely described as extinct here, (except in the Collins Bird Guide - has it recently been rediscovered?). The Goldcrest is also of the race *ellenthallerae*. only found here and on La Palma.

Fuerteventura is the only place in the world where Fuerteventura Chat occurs. Many birders also come here for the desert species, especially because Houbara Bustard and Black-bellied Sandgrouse are much easier to see here than in most other parts of the world where they occur. Fuerteventura Blue Tit (*C.t. degener*) is unique to here and Lanzarote and is considered a separate species by the Dutch Birding Association.

Lanzarote has a similar range of desert species but has now come to be regarded as even better for Houbara Bustard than Fuerteventura. Fantastic collections of seabirds and Eleonora's Falcons breed offshore and species such as Band-rumped (ex-Madeiran) Petrel, White-faced Petrel, Wilson's Petrel and Bulwer's Petrel can be almost guaranteed on well-organised pelagic trips. The Barn Owls here may be of a distinct species (Slender-billed Barn Owl, *Tyto (alba) gracilirostris*, unique to Lanzarote and Fuerteventura). Red-billed Tropicbird is regularly seen in summer and bred for the first time in 2013.

THE CANARY ISLANDS

These islands exceptional for seabirds – best seen from pelagic trips

- Banco de la Concepcion
- Roque del Este
- Alegranza
- Montaña Clara
- La Graciosa

Lanzarote for desert birds especially Houbara Bustards

- airport
- PUERTO DEL CARMEN
- PUERTO DEL ROSARIO
- airport

Fuerteventura for desert birds and Fuerteventura Chat

Eastern Canary Islands for desert species

N ←

0 km 50

La Palma for laurel pigeons and La Palma Blue Tit

SANTA CRUZ DE LA PALMA

Tenerife for most endemics including laurel pigeons, Tenerife Robin, Blue Chaffinch

Tenerife Goldcrest

airport

LAS PALMAS DE GRAN CANARIA

La Gomera for laurel pigeons

SAN SEBASTIAN

airport
LOS CHRISTIANOS

Gran Canaria has no laurel pigeons and Blue Chaffinch is hard to find

airport
PUERTO DE LA ESTACA

El Hierro for El Hierro Blue Tit

Western Canary Islands better for woodland species such as laurel pigeons and Canarian Chiffchaff

3

Southern Tenerife

Attraction

Many visitors will choose to stay in Los Christianos/Playa de Las Americas/Costa Adeje. This has the benefit of being close to the airport and the boats to La Gomera, La Palma and the whale-watching excursions but, with the best sites nearby now out of reach, the birding within a short drive is actually rather limited.

Getting there

These sites are close to the TF-1 which runs around the south of the island between the airport and the main resorts.

Notes

1. El Fraile reservoir, sometimes known as the Embalse de Salema is probably the best wetland on the island, as it invariably supports a collection of ducks, waders, coots, herons, gulls and, sometimes, terns. It has a terrific record for attracting vagrants including regular Nearctic ducks such as Ring-billed Duck and Lesser Scaup. However, when I visited in August 2013 I was completely unable to access the site; every approach I could find was barred by a high gate or fence, as shown on the map. The closest I managed to get was from the town of El Fraile: to get there from the TF-1, take the turning towards Las Galletas until you are passing El Fraile on your right. Turn right at the next roundabout (28.0122N, 16.6637W) and follow this road through El Fraile as far as the football stadium. Drive around the stadium by turning left then right and follow this track as far as you can - probably to the barrier shown (28.0091N, 16.6747W). You have to walk from here; the telegraph poles in the far distance direct you to the reservoir. However, in 2013 I was then confronted by high fences and keep out signs. The bleak, stony habitat around here has formerly been good for Trumpeter Finch, Lesser Short-toed Lark and Barbary Partridge but nowadays you are more likely to see just Berthelot's Pipit, Great Grey Shrike, Hoopoe, Plain Swift, Kestrel and Yellow-legged Gull.

2. The blocked access to the reservoir also makes it much harder to reach the other main birding site, the Punta de la Rasca. As far as I could tell there was no access via the village of El Fraile but it is possible that a route from Palm-Mar may be open to the public, though it would involve a walk of about 2.5km (one-way). The reward would be the chance of some seawatching from near the lighthouse: Cory's Shearwaters are numerous, and sometimes close, and other species such as Bulwer's Petrel and even Baroli's Shearwater have also been seen from here. To get there, try following signs into Palm-Mar then aim for the most southerly street in the development. Google Earth shows a track leading south from there (28.0213N, 16,7002W)) to the lighthouse (28.0012N, 16.6943W) but it may not be open to the public.

3. Most of this corner of Tenerife is a stony desert so any area of greenery could be a magnet for migrants. Two of the most promising sites are the golf courses just west of the airport. The Golf del Sur is signposted from the TF-1; follow the signs until the golf course begins on the left. Almost immediately you should turn right into the car park (28.0398N, 16.6127W) next to a white information centre with big 'Golf del Sur' signs. Looking to the golf course from here you can just about see a water feature which can be good for waders especially Common Sandpiper and Little Ringed Plover and a collection of ducks which on my last visit comprised entirely of about 30 Fulvous Whistling Ducks and a dozen or so Muscovy's. Cattle Egrets are often present and other species recorded here include Spoonbill and crakes. If you walk left from here you can skirt the northern edge of the golf course, checking the greens for migrants and the scrubby desert for Great Grey Shrike and Spectacled Warbler. Alternatively you can walk to the right from the car park to look into the golf course from the road. At passage times and in winter, look for warblers, chats, pipits and wagtails. Red-throated Pipits are regularly seen in

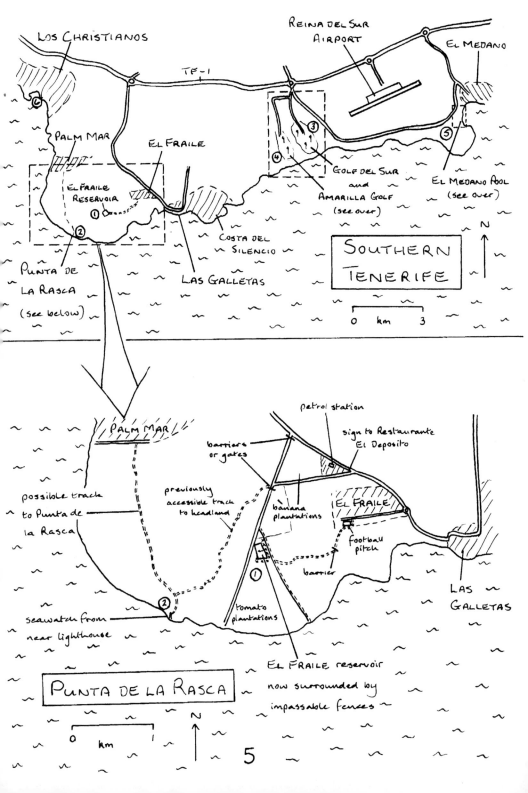

winter. Unless there are a few migrants about, the birding here can be grim but at least you'll see Spanish Sparrows in the car park. Stone Curlews used to be regular to the north of here but this area is now a new resort.

4. Next door to the Golf del Sur is another golf course, the Amarilla, which at least gives you a chance to walk between the greens, rather than along a main road, in search of similar birds. To get there from the Golf del Sur, turn back towards the TF-1 and, at the roundabout before the motorway (28.0477N, 16.6110W), look for a left turn, signposted to Amarilla Golf which takes you into a commercial estate. Aim for the far left corner of this estate (28.0465N, 16.6195W) where you'll find not only a left turn to the golf course but also a decent-sized pool. Check for anything unusual amongst the few egrets, shanks, plovers and sandpipers then continue to the golf clubhouse (28.0317N, 16.6183W). From here you can walk through the greens towards the beach. The small pools just before the clubhouse have had passage waders, Spoonbill and Night Heron.

5. With El Fraile reservoir out of bounds to visitors, the best bet for waders around here is now the El Medano pool. It's a very small lagoon, just inland from a busy beach and usually has only a few birds such as Kentish Plover (which breeds nearby), Dunlin, Sanderling, Turnstone and Whimbrel but there's always a chance of something rarer amongst them. Access is via the road around the back of the airport. There are many car parks along here with access to a beach but the one you want is the most easterly one; the easiest way to find it is to turn off the TF-1 east of the airport following signs to El Medano. As you reach the resort, turn right towards Los Abrigos and park in the first car park on the left (28.0377N, 16.5481W), 500 metres after passing the Hotel Playa Sur. From the car park, take the path past the little building with an aerial, keep straight on at the first 'crossroads' but turn sharp left at the next junction (28.0348N, 16.5472W) along a smaller path until you overlook the pool.

6. The whale-watching trips that depart from the quayside at Los Christianos all offer the chance of getting out into open water closer to where the seabirds are passing so, in theory, you could see species such as Bulwer's Petrel from these boats. In practice, though, I've only ever seen Cory's Shearwater but the views of Short-finned Pilot Whale can be spectacular in themselves.

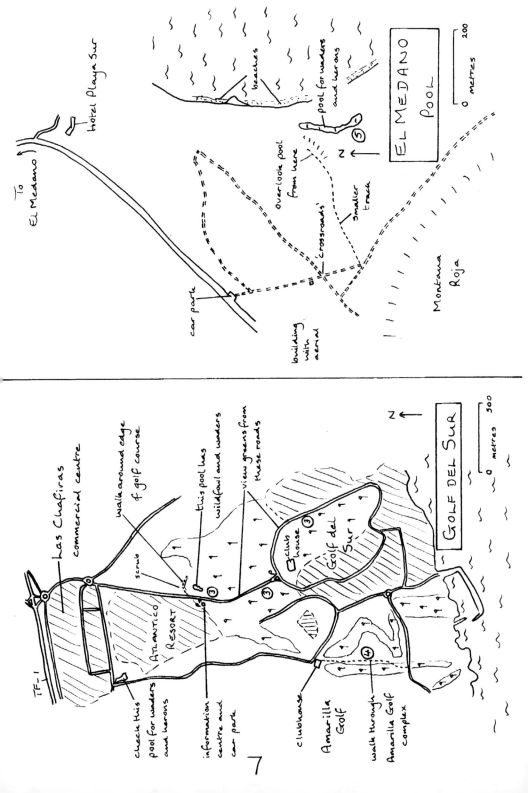

Mount Teide

Attraction

At 3718 metres, Mount Teide is Spain's highest mountain but there is so little vegetation on its upper slopes that it supports very few birds. Lower down, however, the pine forests are home to some unique species and subspecies, most notably Blue Chaffinch, Tenerife Blue Tit and the Tenerife race of Great Spotted Woodpecker.

Getting there

Teide Natural Park is well-signposted from many points of the island; likely routes include the TF82/TF-51 from Los Christianos, via Vilaflor and the TF-21 from Puerto de la Cruz via La Orotava.

Notes

Any area of pine forests along these roads is likely to have the key species plus Canary, Canarian Chiffchaff and Berthelot's Pipit, so any of the picnic sites may be worth a look. Only three such sites are described here.

1. The picnic site at Las Lajas is the number one place in the world for seeing Blue Chaffinch. They are so easy to find here that you will probably at least hear them before you've got out of the car. What makes them so easy to see is the provision of a number of water taps around the picnic areas; each tap has a little trough in which the water is held and so the Blue Chaffinches regularly come down to bathe or drink. They are usually joined by numbers of Canary and the local race of Great Spotted Woodpecker (*Dendrocopus major canariensis*) which is unique to Tenerife and surprisingly abundant (I had at least 8 on my last visit). The Blue Tits (*C.t. teneriffae* - unique to Tenerife, Gran Canaria and La Gomera and already 'split' by the Dutch Birding Association) are usually easy to find and you'll get great views if they come down for water. To get there, take the road north from Vilaflor for 10 km then look for the left turn (28.1915N, 16.6653W) signposted to 'Las Lajas'. As you enter the site, look for a water tap on the right just before the main building on the left as this is particularly popular with the birds. Also, there's a quieter, and possibly better, site further down, on the left, beyond the playground; the nearest pine tree to the little hut shelters a small drinking pool (28.1893N, 16.6657W) which attracts the same species and has better opportunities for photography.

2. If Las Lajas is too busy, there's another site nearby which attracts the same species, away from the crowds. This is the so-called 'leaking pipe' opposite the layby marked with a sign saying Respetemos la Naturaleza. To get there, drive south from Las Lajas, towards Vilaflor until, after 1.2 km, you see a pull-in on the left next to a ruined stone hut. Park here (28.1888N, 16.6570W) in front of the Respetemos la Naturaleza sign. Across the road, look down the hill through the pines to spot a concrete trough-like structure just 30 metres down the slope (28.1886N, 16.6573W). Find a route down to there (no path) and you'll see a pipe running below it, parallel with the road. Birds are attracted to any spot where this pipe is leaking water; just follow it until you see somewhere suitable.

3. The visitor centre at Las Canadas (as opposed to the tourist stop with cafes and restaurants) is often busy with visitors but in the gardens near the car park (28.3040N, 16.5664W) there are a number of water troughs that attract birds to drink and bathe. The commonest birds are usually Canaries, sometimes in flocks of dozens of birds, but Blue Chaffinch and Tenerife Blue Tit have also been recorded. This site is just off the TF-21, 200 metres south of the junction with the TF-24; the El Portillo restaurant at this junction is another place where Blue Chaffinch has been seen.

Mount Teide

- Erjos (see page 13)
- Santiago del Teide
- TF-38
- Chio
- To La Orotava
- El Portillo restaurant
- Las Cañadas information centre — ③
- TF 21
- TF 24
- Las Cañadas restaurants etc.
- Mount Teide
- TF 21
- ① ② Las Lajas for Blue Chaffinch
- TF-21
- Vilaflor
- TF-51
- To Adeje
- To Adeje
- To airport

N ↑

0 — km — 5

Las Lajas

- To Teide
- Sign to Las Lajas
- popular drinking tap
- picnic area ①
- main building
- playground
- drinking pool below pine tree
- open area
- smaller hut
- TF-21
- Small parking area with 'Respetamos la Naturaleza' sign
- concrete block with pipes in
- ruins
- ②
- water may drip from this pipe and attract Blue Chaffinch etc.
- To Vilaflor

Drinking taps in picnic area great for Blue Chaffinch, Canary and Great Spotted Woodpecker

N ↑

0 — metres — 200

9

Northern Tenerife

Attraction

This is the part of the island with laurel forests, the habitat for both laurel pigeons, Tenerife Robin, Tenerife Goldcrest etc. Two of the best areas, near Erjos and around Icod Alto, are treated separately (pages 12 and 14); here we consider other interesting sites in the north.

Getting there

It takes at least an hour to get from Los Christianos to Erjos via the TF-82 which winds around the west of the Island. Alternatively you can take the longer route via the TF-1 motorway around the east of the island. This way you will reach Puerto de la Cruz in about an hour.

Notes

1. Punta de Teno is one of the best seawatching spots on the island and, although out of the way, it is reachable by car. Take the TF-445 road west out of Buenavista and follow it until you reach the lighthouse (28.3421N, 16.9228W). A seawatch from there will produce Cory's Shearwaters with a chance of other species such as Manx and Baroli's Shearwaters, Bulwer's and British Storm Petrels.

2. En route to the point you pass steep seacliffs on which Barbary Falcons breed. One good place to look for them is from the layby (28.3664N, 16.8847W) on the right immediately after the road passes under an arch of rock, 4.1 km from Buenavista. The birds could be on the cliffs on either side of where the road passes through a tunnel. On the far side of the tunnel you may have to drive a while before you find a lay-by (eg 28.3626N, 16.8938W) with enough room to park safely. Park where you can and walk back until you can see the cliff. The fields in the flat coastal area between here and the lighthouse are a well-known site for Rock Sparrows in winter.

3. The Roque de Garachico is a small islet just offshore from the coastal town of Garachico. It is apparently a breeding site for the increasingly rare Baroli's or Macaronesian Shearwater. Garcia del Rey suggests they can be seen from shore on late afternoons throughout the year. The rock is only 350 metres from shore so they shouldn't be too difficult to see but my 2 visits have only produced Cory's Shearwaters.

4. The Ladera de Tigaiga (sometimes called Chanajiga) is an area of laurel forest described by Garcia del Rey as the most accessible and reliable site on Tenerife for the laurel pigeons. I made two visits here in 2013 and saw Bolle's Pigeon but no White-tailed Laurel Pigeons. It is a rather out of the way location but not difficult to find: in Los Realejos, follow signs to Cruz Santa and Palo Blanco. 2.6 km after leaving Palo Blanco take the road to the right (28.3598N, 16.5612W) signposted to Los Llanadas and Zona Recreativa Chanajiga. Follow the most obvious road for 6.3 km as far as the Chanajiga picnic site. Although there are no signs to say so, you must park at the picnic area (28.3440N, 16.5846W) and walk from there; we took our car further down the track but were warned that the area is patrolled and that unauthorised vehicles are given on-the-spot fines, so we turned back. Although you are likely to see birds such as Chaffinch (*tintillon*) and Blue Tit (*teneriffae*) around the picnic areas (and we had Bolle's Pigeon there too), the best laurel areas don't begin until 500 metres down the track and you need to walk further to find a good vantage point so this site can be hard work in the heat of summer. The laurel forests here were great for Tenerife Robin, Tenerife Goldcrest, the Blue Tit and the Chaffinch.

5. The laurel forests in the north-east of the island are certainly good for Bolle's Pigeon but White-tailed Laurel Pigeon is rarely seen here. To get to one of the best sites, leave the TF-1 for La Laguna then follow signs though Las Mercedes until you see a right turn (28.5351N, 16.2724W) to Pico del Ingles. This road ends at the Pico del Ingles mirador (28.5330N, 16.2641W) with views over laurel forests.

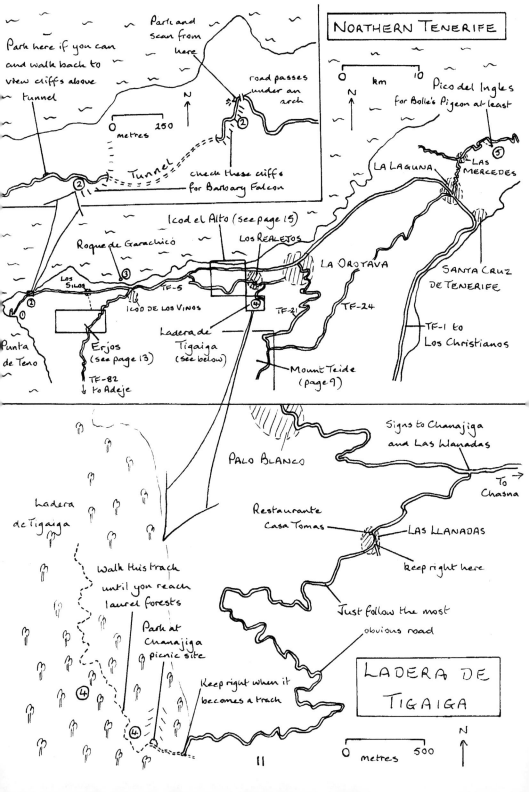

Erjos track and pools (sometimes called Monte del Agua)

Attraction

The track from Erjos to Las Portelas takes you through gorgeous laurel forests containing all the key species of that habitat including both species of laurel pigeon. Although it may be easier to see the pigeons near Icod El Alto (see over), this site gives you a better experience of the laurel forests.

Getting there

The sites described here can be reached from TF-82 as it passes through the village of Erjos. **Note**: There is some confusion over whether the track to sites 1-4 is open to public vehicles. Some visitors have reported seeing 'no entry' signs; others say they have been asked to turn back by wardens but, in 2013, as there were no signs to suggest we couldn't, we twice drove the length of the track with no problem.

Notes

1. Superb laurel forest habitat begins just 850 metres from the main TF-82 road. To get there, drive down the obscure track to the left (28.3257N, 16.8070W) just after the km 16 sign as you leave Erjos, heading north. Follow this track towards, and then beyond, the red and white communications tower until you are under the canopy of prime laurel forest (28.3293N, 16.8103W). From here onwards for the next 10 km you are in the best habitat for birds such as Tenerife Robin, Tenerife Goldcrest, *tintillon* Chaffinch, Tenerife Blue Tit and Canary Islands Chiffchaff although, unless the other species are singing, only the Chiffchaff will be conspicuous. The laurel pigeons will be present but very hard to see from inside the canopy. You get a better chance of seeing them by reaching the following viewpoints.

2. 4.6 km from the start of the track, look for a left-hand bend with a big rock to the right, topped by a rain gauge and with various footpath signs. Park here (28.3295N, 16.8214W) and follow the path to the right of the rock. Be careful, it's steep at first but after just 50 metres, as you get to the far side of the rock, you get a terrific vista over the slopes. Sit here on a little rock to the right of the path (sometimes called Hornbuckle's Rock after the birder who first made it known) and scan for pigeons. In one visit in 1994 I had over 100 sightings of Bolle's Pigeon and a few White-tailed Laurel Pigeon too but recently observers have complained of waiting for hours and just getting a few views of Bolle's Pigeons.

3. As you continue along the track you reach other places where you get great views over the hillsides (eg 28.3310N, 16.8258W and 28.3348N, 16.8260W) so stop to look for laurel pigeons. Scan especially up the steep cliffs above the left side of the road as this is probably your best chance of seeing White-tailed Laurel Pigeon at this site.

4. About 800 metres beyond site 2, look for a drinking tap on the left hand side of the road (approx 28.3321N, 16.8272W). The water here at least attracts the laurel forest passerines such as Chiffchaffs, Blue Tits and Chaffinch and surely the laurel pigeons must sometimes come here to drink but I've waited here several times without joy.

5. Erjos Pools have been described as a potential site for vagrant waterbirds but, more excitingly, David Tomlinson had several Bolle's Pigeons coming here to drink in March 2008 and others have seen them here too. The track to these pools begins (28.3241N, 16.8076W) opposite the bus stop about 250 metres south of the track at site 1. The pools are 600 metres down the track.

6. On being turned back from site 2, David Riddle tried another site by following signs to Cuevas Negras from Los Silos. He describes continuing as far as a red house (possibly 28.3537N, 16.8137W) and seeing White-tailed Laurel Pigeon on the slopes above there (see map on page 10).

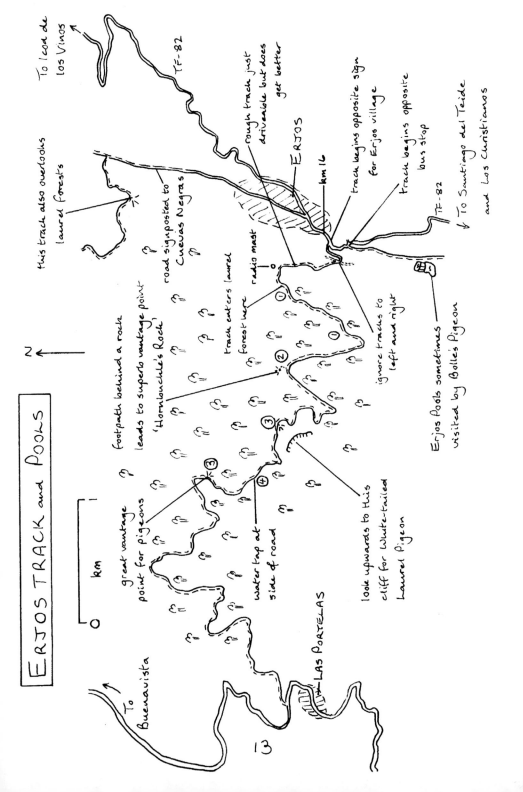

Icod el Alto

Attraction

In 2013 I visited 3 sites where both species of laurel pigeons were easier to see than at either Ladera de Tigaiga or Erjos, all near Icod el Alto. The Ruiz Gorge (site 3) is surely the best place to see both species well.

Getting there

Sites 1 and 2 are accessed directly from the TF-5 'motorway' around the north of the island. For sites 3 and 4, from the TF-5, take the turning to the south between km 48 and 49, signposted to P.I.R.S and La Guancha. Follow this up the steep hill until you reach a T-junction in the centre of La Guancha. Turn left here, signposted to Icod el Alto; sites 3 and 4 are either side of the village.

Notes

1. The Mirador de la Grimona has recently become a popular site for seeing both species of laurel pigeon. It has the benefit of being very easy to find and reach as it is on the TF-5, immediately east of km 43. Coming from the east, as you reach the second of three tunnels you see a sign for the mirador which is then on the right (28.3928N, 16.6089W), immediately after the second tunnel. The habitat here seems most unlikely for laurel pigeons but I scanned up the rocky slope above the mirador and sure enough, within 20 minutes I'd had distant views of both species including perched Bolle's. But since there are almost literally no trees close to the mirador, you're unlikely to ever get close views here.

2. 1.7 km further west, there is a lay-by (28.3916N, 16.6265W) off the TF-5 which is signposted as Barranco de Ruiz. I wondered whether any of the pigeons at site 3 might be visible from here too but the area looks too sparsely vegetated. By scanning from the road around the back of the childrens playground I did see a juvenile Barbary Falcon to the left of the valley and a kestrel to the right.

3. Driving east from La Guancha towards Icod el Alto, before you get to km 9, there is an obvious lay-by and mirador on your left (28.3764N, 16.6262W) overlooking the Barranco de Ruiz. Scan from here and you have a very good chance of seeing either or both laurel pigeons quite distantly over the wooded slopes across the valley. It's also a good spot for seeing Kestrel, Buzzard and Sparrowhawk, all of which are of races endemic to these islands, plus I had a juvenile Barbary Falcon (the bird from site 2?) perched near the car park. From the car park is a short 50 metre fenced walk to a water trough enclosed by trees. Pigeons crashed out of the trees before I could identify them. No birds at all came to the water but there were Chaffinches, Blue Tits, Chiffchaffs and Blackbirds in the trees and Canaries and Sardinian Warblers by the road. To get much better views of the pigeons drive on to the next pull-in (28.3747N, 16.6251W) on the left 200 metres further on. From the side of the road (mind the traffic) you can overlook a narrow wooded gorge in which both species of laurel pigeons are regularly seen. Wait for them to fly then watch where they perch. Even on the far side of the gorge they are close enough to give very good views. It's worth cold-searching whichever bare branches you can see on the far side as the pigeons can sit quietly in full view for hours. On different visits I had up to 12 Bolle's Pigeons but up to 6 White-tailed Laurel Pigeons were seen more consistently. I also had great views of Bolle's Pigeon where the road crosses the gorge; park in front of the defunct Restaurant El Bosque and look down the valley from the bridge. This was good for Blue Tits and Grey Wagtails too.

4. If you continue along that road, through Icod el Alto, you can't fail to see the Mirador El Lance on your left hand side at the far end of the village (28.3849N, 16.6036W). Garcia del Rey describes this as a site for seeing the laurel pigeons but I was sceptical since the nearest trees were miles away. However, sure enough, in the valley far below I soon saw both species around a little wooded valley. But the views here were considerably worse than even the Mirador de Grimona.

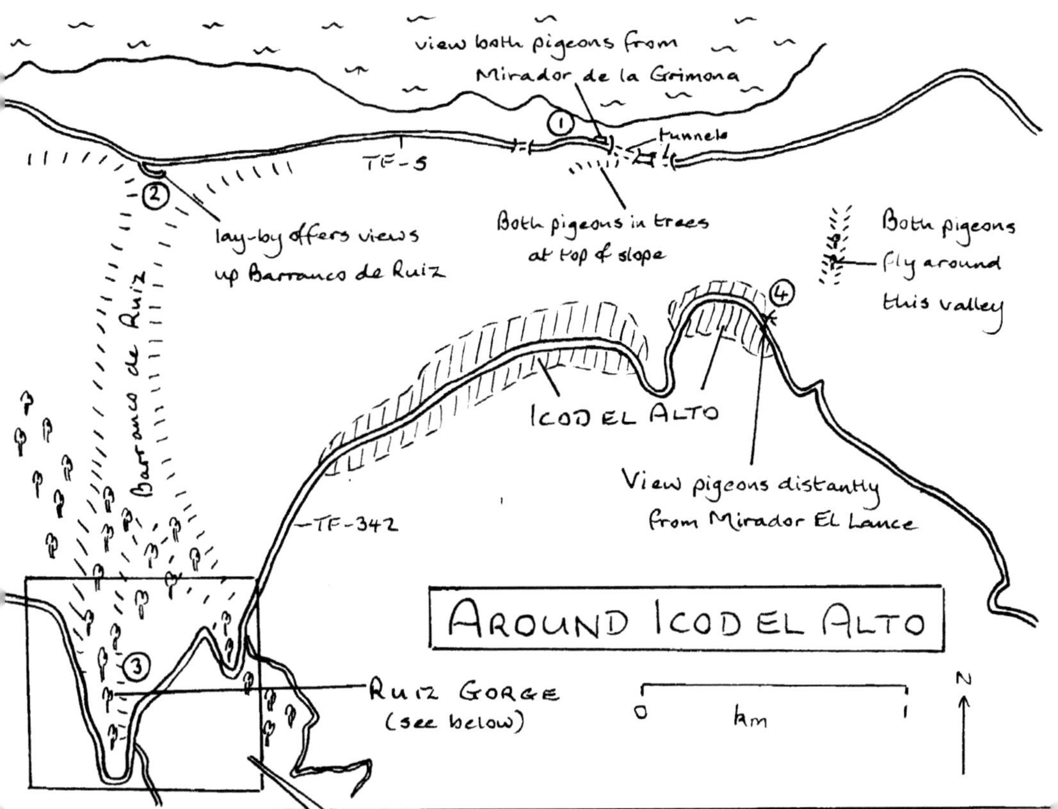
view both pigeons from
Mirador de la Grimona
tunnels
TF-5
1
2
lay-by offers views
up Barranco de Ruiz
Both pigeons in trees
at top of slope
Both pigeons
fly around
this valley
4
Barranco de Ruiz
ICOD EL ALTO
View pigeons distantly
from Mirador El Lance
TF-342
AROUND ICOD EL ALTO
3
RUIZ GORGE
(see below)
0
km
1
N

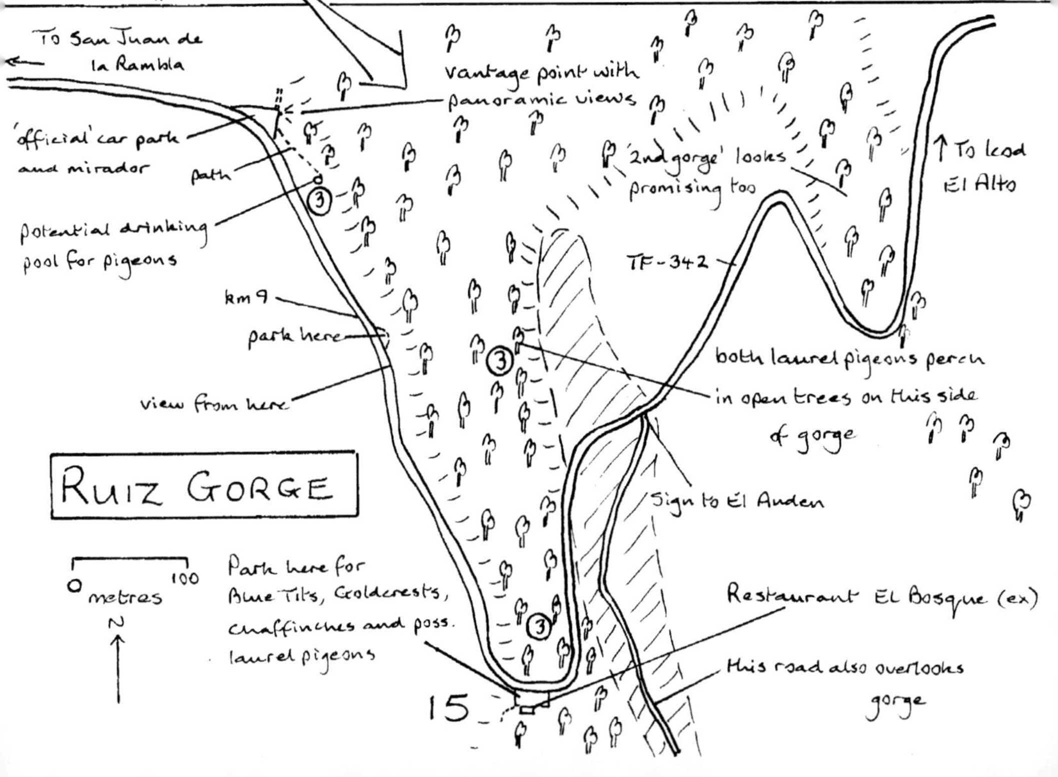
To San Juan de
la Rambla
vantage point with
panoramic views
'official' car park
and mirador
path
3
potential drinking
pool for pigeons
'2nd gorge' looks
promising too
To Icod
El Alto
TF-342
km 9
park here
view from here
both laurel pigeons perch
in open trees on this side
of gorge
RUIZ GORGE
Sign to El Anden
0
metres
100
N
Park here for
Blue Tits, Goldcrests,
chaffinches and poss.
laurel pigeons
Restaurant El Bosque (ex)
This road also overlooks
gorge

La Gomera

Attraction

Many birdwatchers make at least a day trip here from Tenerife, partly because laurel pigeons are easier to see here but also because the ferry en route offers a chance to see seabirds such as Bulwer's Petrel and Baroli's (=Macaronesian) Shearwater.

Getting there

Two ferry companies operate boats to La Gomera from Los Christianos but there are only limited viewing opportunities from the faster boats run by Fred Olsen. Instead you should take the first morning ferry with Naviera Armas, returning on the last boat back.

Notes

1. The best place for seeing both species of laurel pigeon is along the CV-14 road through the Garajonay Natural Park which connects the Carretera del Norte with the Carretera del Sur. The map shows the location of a number of laybys from which you can scan for pigeons. In 2013 we saw both species from all of them, with lots of sightings altogether. The best view of perched White-tailed Pigeon was by looking back down the road from the Mirador de El Rejo (28.1252N, 17.2066W), in exposed branches below the road. We also had Tenerife Goldcrest at two of the viewpoints.

2. We also had both laurel pigeons by walking to the Mirador del Bailadero from the lay-by (28.1230N, 17.2103W) to the left of the road 500 metres before you reach the road to Monte del Cedro. As you walk down the steps you overlook a hillside across which both species sometimes fly but the best views were from the viewpoint before the steps, just 60 metres from the lay-by. Looking back from here towards the road you see a tree-covered slope with many bare branches. We had a White-tailed Pigeon perched briefly in those branches.

3. The track to Monte del Cedro is well-signposted from the CV-14. You can drive or walk this track for many kilometres through excellent laurel forest habitat with *tintillon* Chaffinch, Tenerife Goldcrest, Tenerife Blue Tit and lots of Canarian Chiffchaff. Both laurel pigeons are here too but because of the closed canopy you are more likely to hear them than see them: White-tailed Laurel Pigeon song starts with a deep 'mooo', followed by regular 'double-moos'; Bolle's Pigeon is more reminiscent of Wood Pigeon but deeper and rather subdued, as if singing through a curtain.

4. The woodland opens out at Monte del Cedro so there's a chance to scan for pigeons here. In 2013 we didn't spend much time looking for them but instead enjoyed close views of Canaries, in the fig tree opposite the balcony of the cafe (28.1373N, 17.2151W), and *tintillon* Chaffinches around the car park (28.1324N, 17.2143W) back up the road.

5. Both laurel pigeons have previously been reported from this bar (28.1345N, 17.1940W) but it is now closed and barriers across the drive make it difficult to park there.

6. The *baroli* form of Little Shearwater is now widely regarded as a separate species, Baroli's or Macaronesian Shearwater. It appears to be declining at an alarming rate but the ferry crossing between Tenerife and La Gomera still offers a chance to see them. We had good views of 2 birds on the return ferry in mid August 2013. We also had several views of Bulwer's Petrel on both legs of the journey. Cory's Shearwaters are of course numerous and British Storm Petrels are sometimes seen too.

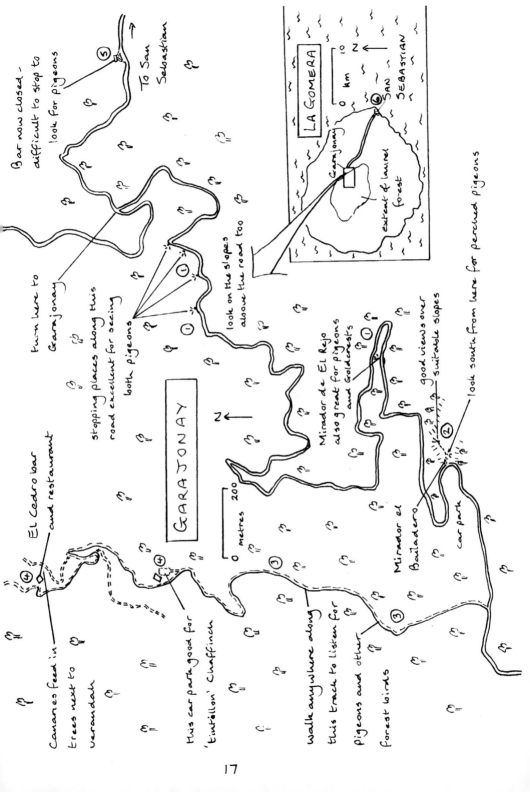

La Palma

Attraction

The laurel pigeons are even easier to see here than on La Gomera and many birdwatchers will now be drawn to the island because the Blue Tit here has been recognised by some (eg the Dutch Birding Association) as a distinct species, unique to La Palma. The local Chaffinch may soon gain similar status and the Goldcrest is different from the one on Tenerife and La Gomera.

Getting there

Ferries go to Santa Cruz de la Palma on most days from Los Christianos, Tenerife. The journey can take up to 6 hours, depending on the winds and currents. Or you can fly here from most of the islands.

Notes

1. The most famous place for seeing the pigeons is at Los Tilos. From Santa Cruz de la Palma, find the main road to the north (LP-1) by following signs to Barlovento or Los Sauces. Just after passing km 21, you'll see a turning to the left (28.7963N, 17.7706W) signposted to Los Tilos. Turn left here, then left again after 1 km and follow this road all the way to the visitor centre where the road ends. By looking up from this car park (28.7898N, 17.8021W) we had lots of views of pigeons of both species but mostly rather distant flight views. A better place to scan for pigeons is from the car park (approx 28.7927N, 17.7968W) 800 metres back down the road. This overlooks a steep valley, offering closer views including birds perched in bare branches on the far slope. However, we had our best views by returning to the visitor centre in late afternoon when several Bolle's Pigeon came to feed on the fruiting trees above the picnic area and could be watched in the canopy at close range. The trees around the picnic area were also good for the distinctive Chaffinches and Blue Tits; the Chaffinches come for scraps around the visitor centre.

2. One trip report (by E.J.Alblas on Surfbirds.com) suggested that the nearby valley of Cubo de la Galga was a better bet for White-tailed Pigeon. This is found just north of the km 16 marker on the way back to Santa Cruz, marked by signs, a car park (28.7670N, 17.7698W) and an information centre. He twice walked for 3 km up the valley from here and although he heard plenty of pigeons of both species and saw a few Bolle's Pigeons he had only 4 flight sightings of White-tailed Laurel Pigeon and one bird perched. I spent little time here as I wanted somewhere where I could film the pigeons without carrying the camera too far.

3. The Mirador de las Hesperides (28.7722N, 17.7663W), just north of km 17 and the El Valle tunnel, offers good views over potential habitat but I saw little from here.

4. A much better site that I can recommend was the track (28.7709N, 17.7706W) that heads inland immediately south of the El Valle tunnel. The first 100 metres of that track overlook a wooded slope on both sides of the main road and I saw both laurel pigeons from here. The views of White-tailed Laurel Pigeons perching in trees just across the valley were closer than at Los Tilos but, even better, I also had one perched briefly in the open on the near side of the valley.

5. We searched in vain for the 'airport pools' described in Clarke and Colllins and recommended in Leo Boon's video. Once a great site for waders, these seem to have been subsumed either by an expansion of the airport or by the planting of vegetation.

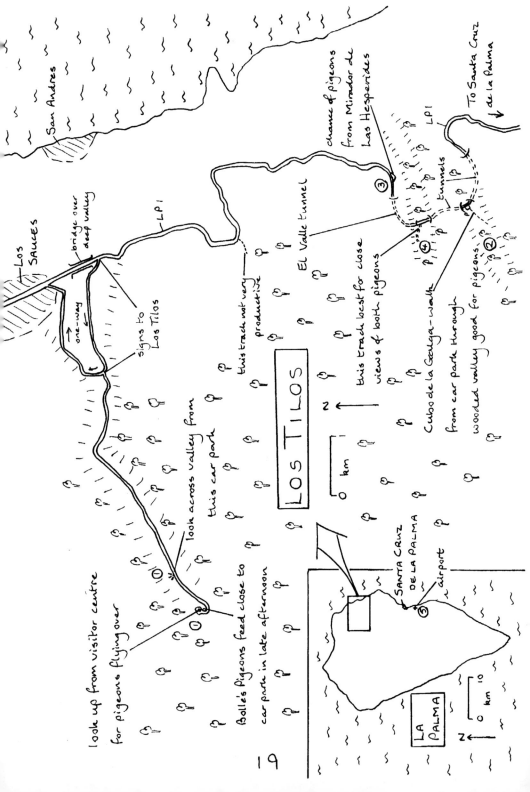

Northern Fuerteventura

Attraction

The south of the island (see page 30) seems to have become more popular with visiting birdwatchers but the north still has the greatest densities of Houbara Bustard, the best-known sites for Fuerteventura Chat and Fuerteventura Blue Tit and the full range of desert species. Los Molinos, the Tindaya Plain and Caleta de Fuste are all in the north of the island but are treated separately (pages 24 to 29).

Getting there

These areas are within easy reach of the resorts of Caleta de Fuste and Corralejo. The roads throughout the island are excellent.

Notes

1. The Barranco de Rio Cabras, sometimes called Willis's Barranco, became famous as a place where birders could arrive at the airport, see Fuerteventura Chat and leave again within a couple of hours. However, the road past the entrance to the valley has been turned into a motorway with no suitable stopping place. Richard Bonser reports that the upper part of the barranco (28.4884N, 13.9274W) can still be accessed, and the chat located, from the FV-225 road to Triquivijate, about 500 metres south of the junction with the FV-20 to Puerto del Rosario. He had a pair of chats downstream from the road and, surprisingly, a Laughing Dove upstream from there.

2. The area around Triquivijate has high densities of Houbara Bustard and Cream-coloured Courser is regularly seen here, though I have failed to find either species on my visits. One site worth visiting though is the pool at Rosa del Taro. Take the FV-225 north from Triquivijate until, after 5.7 km (28.4549N, 13.9607W), you see a pool on your left opposite a sign saying Atalaya de la Rosa del Taro. In August 2013 it was completely dry but, when wet, it supports a few wildfowl, such as Coot, and waders and attracts a few passerines to the surrounding bushes. This is also a well-known site for Black-bellied Sandgrouse coming to drink, mid-morning.

3. The update to my previous book includes a report from an uncredited observer that Houbara Bustard, Cream-coloured Courser and Black-bellied Sandgrouse were seen regularly in August 1995 on the 'orange-coloured plain just north of Antigua'. I checked here in August 2013 and, sure enough, had fantastic views of both Houbara Bustard and Black-bellied Sandgrouse on 2 visits. These sightings were just north of km 18 on the FV-20 north of Antigua, where a track to the left (28.4419N, 14.0065W) leads to what look like sand pits. Scan either from this track or from the main road close to the brow of the hill, looking for Houbara in the bushier areas and sandgrouse around the banks of the 'sandpits'. Google Earth shows these 'sandpits' to be simple reservoirs so this is a likely drinking spot for the sandgrouse.

4. The hills and valleys around the pretty little town of Betancuria have more trees than most other parts of the island. Hence a small population of Canaries has become established here, especially in the trees to the south of town, though they can also be found in the town itself. This is also one of the best sites on the island for Fuerteventura Blue Tit (*C.t. degener*), regarded by some as a seperate species and confined to this island and Lanzarote.

NORTHERN FUERTEVENTURA

ANTIGUA PLAIN

0 metres 300

- HB = Houbara Bustard
- BBS = B-bellied Sandgrouse

view from road...
...or from track
FV-20
sandy bungalow
km 18
"sand pits"

- Correlejo
- El Cotillo
- Tindaya Plain (see page 29)
- La Oliva
- Los Molinos (see page 27)
- Puerto del Rosario
- FV-225
- Barranco de Rio Cabras ①
- Rosa del Tarq ②
- FV-20
- Antigua Plain
- ③ Triquivijate
- ④
- Antigua
- Caleta
- ⑤ ⑥ Betancuria
- Las Peñitas (see page 23)
- Caleta de Fuste area (see page 25)
- Tuineje
- Rosa de Catalina Garcia (see page 23) ⑦

0 km 5

N ↑

21

5. Another place to look for the Blue Tits is in the valley of Las Penitas. Drive south from Betancuria on the FV-30 for 4 km to the village of Vega de Rio Palma. As the main road passes through the village, take a turning to the right (28.3937N, 14.0757W), signposted to 'La Vega...', and follow this for 1.2 km to the far side of the village where a bridge crosses the valley. Park by the bridge (28.3936N, 14.0879W) and walk down the river bed. The valley is relatively well-vegetated and usually has a few small pools so, in addition to the Blue Tits you might find some migrants and this is a particularly good area for Turtle Doves. We also had Spectacled Warbler and Fuerteventura Chat where the slopes were scrubbier and flushed a covey of Barbary Partridge from the rocky slopes. If you keep to the right of the valley, after passing an area of tamarisks you will overlook a small reservoir, the Embalse de Las Penitas, though on our visit this was completely dry.

6. If you follow the FV-30 south for a further 2 km you see a mirador on the right which overlooks Las Penitas. The scraps left in this car park (28.3870N, 14.0924W) not only attract ridiculously tame Berthelot's Pipits but also almost equally fearless Ravens. Throughout the Canary Islands these are of the north African race *Corvus corax tingitanus* which is sometimes considered to be a separate species (African Common Raven). This is also one of the best spots on the island to look for Egyptian Vulture, though we only had Kestrel (race *dacotiae*) and Buzzard (race *insularum*).

7. One of the best wetlands on Fueteventura is the reservoir at Rosa de Catalina Garcia. In the past it has been a regular site for species such as Coot, Black-winged Stilt and Ruddy Shelduck (which has bred here) and a drinking site for Black-bellied Sandgrouse (landing on the far side of the pool between 9 and 10 am - Steve Lister). In visits over several years Frances Gatens has also had Spoonbill, Osprey, 13 species of waders, 11 species of duck (including Blue-winged Teal, Ring-necked Duck and Lesser Scaup) and migrant passerines including Whinchat, Common Stonechat and Wheatear. However, in August 2013 it was completely dry. To get there, take the FV-20 south from Tuineje towards Gran Tarajal then, after about 5km, look for a track to the left (28.3000N, 14.0258W), between km markers 36 and 37. It looks like the drive to a little white roadside house but continues past here towards a couple of palm trees. Look for a fork in the track that takes you to the right of the palm trees and continue for about a kilometre until you are overlooking the reservoir. There is a hide at the far side, though it may be locked.

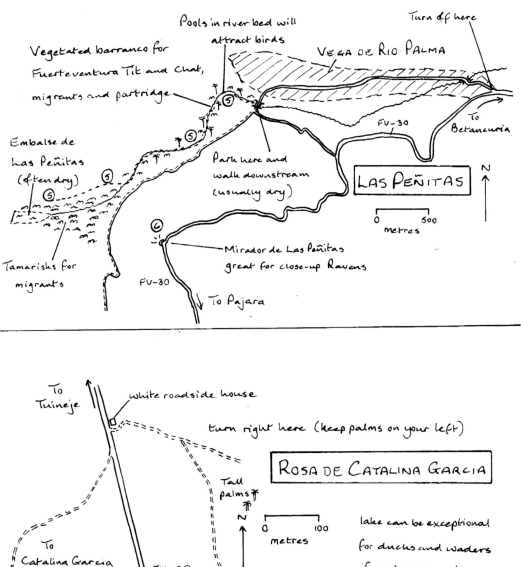

Around Caleta de Fuste

Attraction

Probably the resort of choice for birders staying in the north of the island. Most of the island's desert birds, including the chat, can be found nearby and there are good sites for waders and Egyptian Vulture.

Getting there

The resort is just 6.5 km south of the airport down the FV-2

Notes

1. There are a number of places along the resort promenade where the tourists feed monkey nuts to Barbary Ground Squirrels but the feeding sites (eg at 28.4027N, 13.8534W) along the cycle track to the north of the resort also attract Trumpeter Finches, sometimes at very close range.

2. The maturing trees in the resort itself provide enough greenery to attract migrants such as warblers and flycatchers. It is likely that the best areas for migrants will be the golf courses that have recently been created at the southern end of the resort.

3. Despite the development of a new main road running through it, towards Triquivijate, the area to the north-west of the resort is still good for desert species. Follow the road for 2 km then turn right (28.4120N, 13.8864W), signposted to 'Depuradora' (sewage works). The compound behind the sewage works is a rubbish tip which in 2013 had a pair of Fuerteventura Chat plus Spanish Sparrows and Berthelot's Pipits; Black-bellied Sandgrouse and a Cream-coloured Courser flew over. Continue along the track past the depuradora and you will overlook a barranco on your left. The barranco has at least one permanent pool (only Common Sandpiper in 2013) and has Spectacled Warbler and a chance of more chats. An area of flat ground (28.4179N, 13.8927W) beyond the barranco is invariably attractive to Egyptian Vultures, Buzzards and Ravens so I suspect it may be an artificial feeding site; it's certainly one of the best places on the island to see Egyptian Vulture (I had up to 4 birds). Another area worth exploring for coursers, sandgrouse and Trumpeter Finch is around the ruined buildings just past km 1.

4. The saltpans at Salinas del Carmen are good for waders but they are easily disturbed by visitors to the Museo del Sal. I recommend driving past the museo and finding the road to the left down to the shore in front of the village (28.3659N, 13.8718W). From there you can get better views of the birds on the deep pools between the car park and the saltpans. These tend to attract more birds (Sanderling, Dunlin, shanks, sandpipers) than the saltpans themselves. You can also walk out from here to the coastal lagoon which is good for different birds such as Grey Plover, Whimbrel, Turnstone and Sandwich Tern.

5. The Barranco de la Torre is widely considered to be the best site on the island for Fuerteventura Chat. With patience, the chats can be found almost wherever you look in this valley. There are several ways to access the barranco but the easiest and most rewarding is by following the road through Salinas del Carmen until you reach the tower at the coastal end of the barranco. Drive past the old building ('prohibido el paso' refers to the buildings, not the track) then look for a track off to the right (28.3565N, 13.8786W) up the barranco. Park prettily and walk inland from there (don't leave any valuables in your car). Apart from being famous for the chat, this part of the valley often has pools that support waterbirds including herons such as Spoonbills and ducks such as Ruddy Shelduck.

6. The barranco can also be accessed 5km further inland by taking the road signposted to Los Alares. As this road begins, look for a track to the right (28.3729N, 13.9291W) towards a settlement with palm trees. Follow this as far as the barranco (chats and Spectacled Warblers) and look out for Black-bellied Sandgrouse coming to drink at the pools (28.3769N, 13.9267W) by the palm trees.

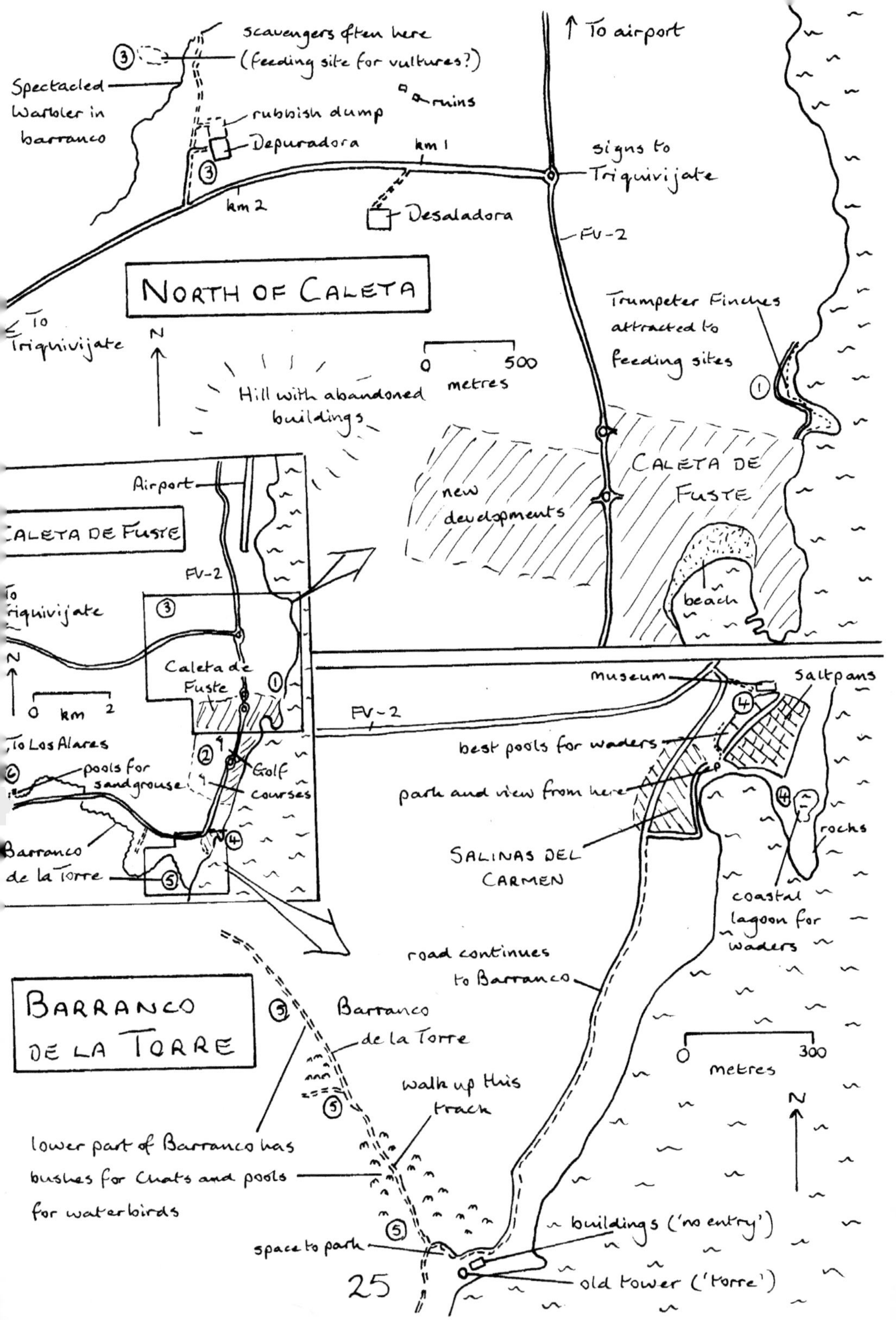

scavengers often here (feeding site for vultures?)
Spectacled Warbler in barranco
rubbish dump
Depuradora
ruins
To airport
km 1
km 2
signs to Triquivijate
Desaladora
FV-2
NORTH OF CALETA
To Triquivijate
N
0 500 metres
Hill with abandoned buildings
Trumpeter Finches attracted to feeding sites
new developments
CALETA DE FUSTE
beach
Airport
CALETA DE FUSTE
FV-2
To Triquivijate
N
0 km 2
Caleta de Fuste
To Los Alares
pools for sandgrouse
Golf courses
Barranco de la Torre
Museum
Saltpans
FV-2
best pools for waders
park and view from here
rocks
SALINAS DEL CARMEN
coastal lagoon for waders
road continues to Barranco
BARRANCO DE LA TORRE
Barranco de la Torre
0 300 metres
walk up this track
lower part of Barranco has bushes for Chats and pools for waterbirds
space to park
buildings ('no entry')
old tower ('Torre')

Los Molinos

Attraction

The largest body of water on Fuerteventura and the only one sure to have at least some water, even in high summer. As well as dozens of Coot and Black-winged Stilt there are now good numbers of Ruddy Shelduck here and its one of the best places for migrant ducks and waders. The surrounding areas have all the island's desert species including the chat and Houbara Bustard.

Getting there

The best point of access is from Las Parcelas. To get there, turn west from the FV-20 towards Betancuria, then north on the FV-207 towards Tefia. After 3.5 km take the FV-221 to the left, signposted to Las Parcelas and Los Molinos. The turn-off to the dam is from the last bend in the village of Las Parcelas, on a track to the left (28.5304N, 14.0410W) before a goat-shed.

Notes

1. Before you even get to the reservoir, check around the goat sheds in the village for Trumpeter Finch and Lesser Short-toed Lark. The barranco below the dam is a regular haunt of Fuerteventura Chat.

2. Park at the dam (28.5128N, 14.0314W) and walk along the east side of the reservoir. There will be Coot and Ruddy Shelduck on the water and Black-winged Stilts and other waders around the shore. You really need a telescope to check everything thoroughly. Past visitors here have included Ring-necked Duck, Red-knobbed Coot, 3 species of crake and Allen's Gallinule but it seems the Marbled Duck that used to breed here have now gone. Don't get too excited by the sight of a hide near the path - it was locked in 2013. Birds seen from the path are likely to include Lesser Short-toed Lark, Great Grey Shrike and Hoopoe.

3. In my experience the easiest place to find Fuerteventura Chat is around the coastal hamlet of Los Molinos. Upstream from here is a barranco with breeding chats and Spectacled Warblers and this is another good spot for seeing Egyptian Vulture. However, you will often see the chats around the car park (28.5426N, 14.0631W) at the end of the road; for some reason they seem to be attracted to the rubbish bins on the left just before the car park. You'll probably see them before you've even left the car.

4. The route to Los Molinos reservoir described in my previous book is no longer recommended as a way to see the waterbirds (because the water level has shrunk and access is anyway more difficult than at site 2) but it does get you to an area that can be great for desert birds. From Tefia take the FV-207 south towards Los Llanos until, 400 metres after km post 8, you see a broad track to the right (28.5037N, 14.0051W) just before some 'no overtaking' signs. After 1.4 km, this track meanders around the left hand side of a house, through two sets of gates. Keep going, aiming for the blue container sheds ahead and park there (28.5035N, 14.0256W). This used to overlook the top end of the reservoir which could then be reached on foot but instead I now recommend it as a place to scan for desert birds; look especially in the stony area behind the containers as this is a regular site for Cream-coloured Couser and Black-bellied Sandgrouse. You might get better views of these birds by retracing your steps and turning left up a track (28.5025N, 14.0229W) after 250 metres. Others have had Houbara Bustard at Los Molinos but I don't know exactly where.

Los Molinos

Upper map:

- Puertito de Los Molinos ③
- barranco for chats and Egyptian Vulture
- Fuerteventura Chat where road ends
- goat-shed (look for T Finch and LST Lark)
- turn left as road bends to right
- Las Parcelas ⓪
- FV-221
- Tefia
- FV-207
- follow track to reservoir
- ① Fuerteventura Chat in barranco
- Los Molinos reservoir (see below)
- ②
- ④
- km 8 — two isolated palm trees
- 'no overtaking' signs
- N ↑
- 0 — 1 km

Lower map (Los Molinos detail):

- dam
- park by ruined building
- ② follow this path
- hide (often locked) ②
- check reservoir for ducks and waders
- in wet years reservoir may extend to here
- blue freight containers
- no obvious path from here
- ④ goat sheds
- stony plain great for coursers and sandgrouse
- ④ view from track....
- ....or from behind containers
- house
- follow track around house
- 0 — 500 metres
- N ↑

27

Tindaya Plain

Attraction

This area has the highest density of Houbara Bustards on Fuerteventura and is also good for Cream-coloured Courser and Black-bellied Sandgrouse.

Getting there

The area is in the triangle between El Cotillo, La Oliva and Tindaya and can be reached from each of those towns as described below.

Notes

1. Drive into El Cotillo until you see the football stadium on your right. Look for a left turn signposted to Playa Piedra-Playa which points you to a track (28.6809N, 14.0081W) running out of town, parallel to the coast. In 2013 this soon became rather rough so I didn't fancy following it for more than 3.5 kilometres. Even so, I did see birds such as Trumpeter Finch and Lesser Short-toed Lark and a party of Black-bellied Sandgrouse which looked as if they were coming to a drinking site somewhere near the ruin (28.6594N, 14.0083W) opposite the villa. (Incidentally, the track which passes closest to the beaches is the one that eventually joins up with the track from site 3, though I can't vouch for whether it is drivable along its entire length.)

2. As you leave La Oliva on the road towards El Cotillo, look for a track (28.6233N, 13.9421W) up a steep bank directly opposite the last house in the town. Follow this for just over a kilometre to a farmstead with palm trees and some lines of fig trees. This site, known as Rosa de los Negrines became famous in 1994 when I announced that I'd seen up to 13 Houbara Bustards coming to roost here every evening and they could be watched at close range if you stayed in your vehicle (eg from 28.6353N, 13.9537W). Since then many birders have seen these bustards but it turns out they use this site not for roosting but for feeding on the fallen figs. Hence it was most attractive to them in late summer and autumn and visitors at other times often missed them. Recently however it has been described as a 'former site for bustards' and when I checked in August 2013 I didn't see any bustards in the evening. I'm not sure why the bustards have gone, except that the desert areas around here have become greatly denuded of other vegetation - and the bustards love the bushier parts of the desert. I notice that beyond the farmstead a huge area has been fenced off as a bustard reserve. Hopefully, within that area, goats will be kept at bay and bushes will be allowed to grow so, hopefully, this will again become a great place to see the bustards. If they are there, the views you get are so good it is always worth at least one evening visit to check it out.

3. Another site for the bustards was given in my original book; an uncredited observer described finding both Houbara and coursers 'about 1 km from Tindaya on the tarmac track to Punta Paso Chico' in August 1995. I explored this track in 2013 and was impressed by the quality of the habitat and the ease of accessibility. The tarmac track takes you though 4 km of superb desert and other tracks leading from here give you a massive area to cruise along in search of bustards, coursers and sandgrouse from the vehicle. The highlight of my 2013 trip was coming across a Houbara Bustard right next to the tarmac track, curiously 1 km from Tindaya, exactly as described. I returned here twice more and had a Houbara (presumably the same bird) each time. Surely it's not a coincidence that this spot (28.6022N, 13.9984W) is marked by a small copse of fig trees. I suggest this is another place where Houbaras (well, 1 at least) are attracted to fallen figs. The area was also great for other desert birds such as Lesser Short-toed Lark and Trumpeter Finch.

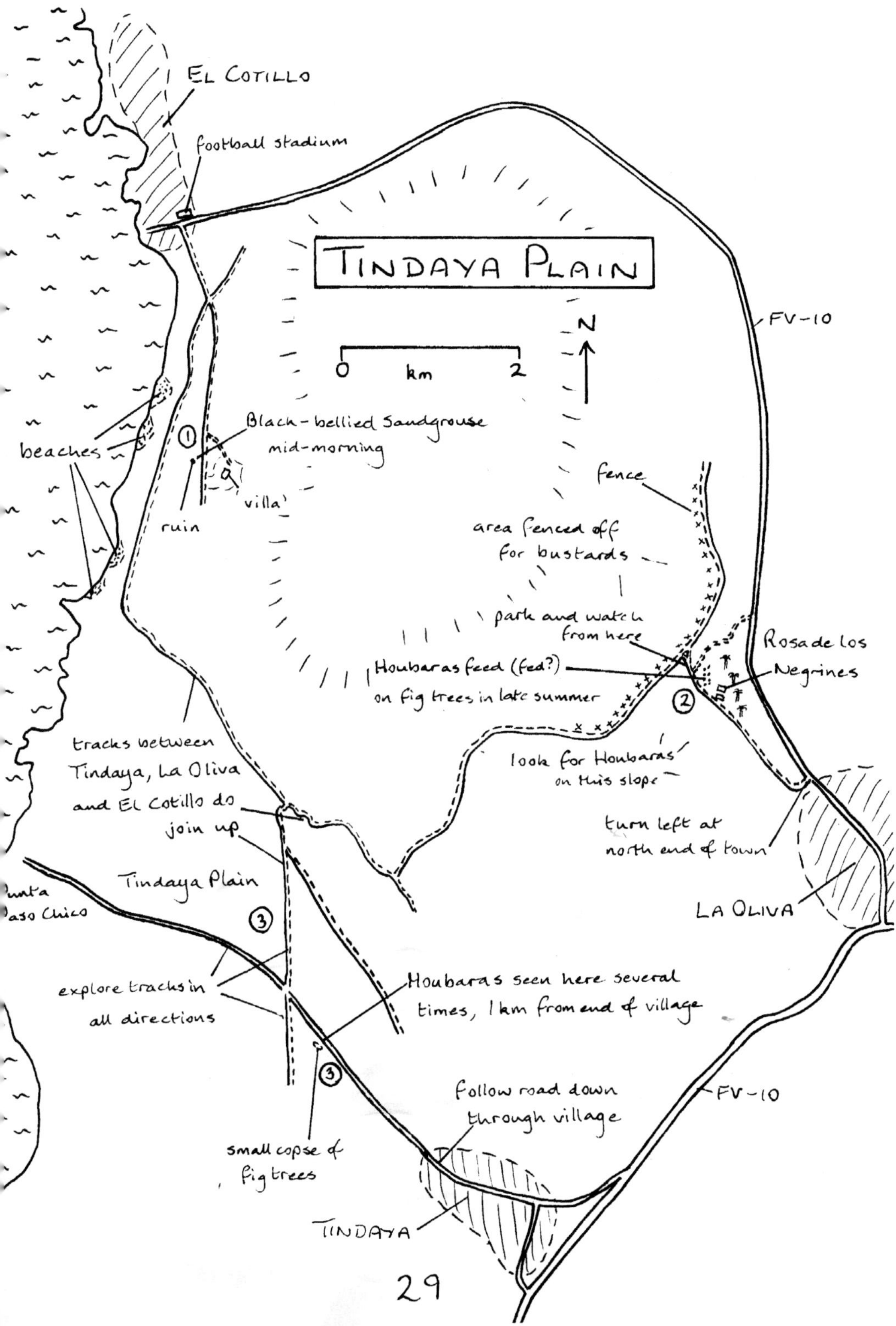

Tindaya Plain

EL COTILLO

football stadium

0 — km — 2

N ↑

FV-10

beaches

① Black-bellied Sandgrouse mid-morning

ruin villa

fence

area fenced off for bustards

park and watch from here

Houbaras feed (fed?) on fig trees in late summer

② Rosa de los Negrines

tracks between Tindaya, La Oliva and El Cotillo do join up

look for Houbaras on this slope

turn left at north end of town

LA OLIVA

Punta Paso Chico

Tindaya Plain

③ explore tracks in all directions

Houbaras seen here several times, 1km from end of village

③ small copse of fig trees

follow road down through village

FV-10

TINDAYA

29

Costa de Jandia (Southern Fuerteventura)

Attraction

This part of the island offers all the desert species, including the chat and Houbara Bustard but is also a much better bet for migrants since the beaches support significantly larger numbers of waders and there are relatively well-wooded areas here where migrants and wintering birds tend to concentrate. There are free-flying exotic birds here too and the area is exceptionally good for Black-bellied Sandgrouse.

Getting there

From the north, just continue down the FV-2 following signs to Morro Jable until you reach La Lajita.

Notes

1. In and around the Oasis Park zoo at La Lajita there are lush trees that could be good for migrants and also support a number of free-flying exotic species which have no doubt originated from the zoo. To get there, follow the main FV-2 through La Lajita and then turn right (28.1858N, 14.1584W), following signs for the park entrance. This leads to a car park. From there, if the gates are open you can walk under the main road to where the camel safaris begin (28.1864N, 14.1563W); explore from there, especially to the right (west). (If the gates are closed you can reach the same areas by walking back down the entrance road and crossing the main road). Around the car park I had at least 6 Red-vented Bulbuls, at least 6 Lavender Waxbills and at least 2 unidentified parrots, all free-flying. I also had all-too-brief views of what looked like a Northern Oriole. Was it another escape from the zoo or a genuine transatlantic migrant? Across the road there were a few Laughing Doves amongst many Collared Doves on the track parallel to the road. A small sewage pond had Common Sandpiper and Great Grey Shrike. Richard Bonser has walked further west from here and had Fuerteventura Chat in the next barranco.

2. On either side of the main road through Costa Calma is a relatively substantial area of woodland (eg at 28.1618N, 14.2287W) which is good for migrants (I had Bonelli's Warbler and Chiffchaff) and wintering birds (eg thrushes, robins and, sometimes, Yellow-browed Warblers). As at many places along this coast, the beach has many intertidal pools or lagoons which are worth checking for gulls, terns and waders but you have to be there before the sunbathers.

3. The area between Costa Calma and La Pared (Ista de la Pared) is exceptional for Houbara Bustard and sandgrouse and is described overleaf.

4. Another good site for migrant passerines is in and around the grounds of the Hotel Los Gorriones (or Melia Gorriones). This is also an exceptional site for waders. At low tide they are in pools along the beach (along with gulls and terns including regular Slender-billed Gulls) and at high tide they roost on the clifftops. To see them, follow signs from the FV-2 to Playa de la Barca, then, when you arrive at the Hotel Garriones (28.1377N, 14.2468W), turn right into the hotel area but follow signs to 'lagoon' until you are driving along the clifftop. One good wader roost is around the car park (28.1290N, 14.2504W) 900 metres from the hotel; I had over 200 birds, mostly Kentish Plover and Sanderling. Houbara Bustard has been seen in the barranco opposite the turn off from the main road.

5. Further down the coast, at Morro Jable, is another zoo with lush vegetation and free-flying exotics. In particular there is a colony of Monk Parakeets which are easy to view. As you arrive in Morro Jable, look for a roundabout with a sculpture of two wrestlers (28.0499N, 14.3292W); park as soon as you can after that. The parakeets are numerous and noisy on both sides of the road opposite the Stella Canaris zoo. Yellow-browed warbler has been seen in the gardens of the zoo. Once again the coast near here has lagoons where waders might be found, if you get there before the sunbathers.

COSTA DE JANDIA

N ↑

0 — 1 — 2 — 3 km

- Istmo de la Pared (see over) — great for desert species
- La Pared
- Oasis Park Zoo has free-flying exotics, Laughing Doves and migrants
- ① La Lajita
- FV-605
- ② Costa Calma has areas of trees good for migrants
- Hotel Melia Gorriones also attracts migrants
- waders and gulls occur on pools at low tide
- cliff top here great for roosting waders at high tide
- more pools for waders and gulls
- ③
- ④
- FV-2
- Risco del Paso beach
- Pico de la Zarza
- steep cliffs
- Monk Parakeets in trees outside Stella Canaris Zoo
- Stella Canaris
- ⑤ Morro Jable
- Lighthouse
- check coastline for waders

31

Istmo de la Pared

Attraction

An area of sandy and stony desert on which birders have had fantastic views of Houbara Bustard, especially in spring when they are displaying. Coursers are also seen regularly and Black-bellied Sandgrouse are exceptionally numerous, especially around their regular drinking site at La Pared.

Getting there

These areas can be accessed either directly from Costa Calma or via the road from Costa Calma to La Pared.

Notes

1. All the desert species have been found by taking a track from Costa Calma. To get there, turn right at the roundabout (28.1598N, 14.2314W) at the western end of the resort, just past a petrol station with a curved roof. Follow this road past El Palmeral shopping centre then, after the road bends left, aim for the pylon at the top of the road. In 2003 Richard Bonser drove for 5 km up this track (from 28.1652N, 14.2339W) and found Houbara Bustard, Black-bellied Sandgrouse, Barbary Partridge, Stone-Curlew, Trumpeter Finch and Lesser Short-toed Lark. On my visit I chickened out of driving through the ridges of sand 500 metres up the track so instead I walked as far as the 'crossroads' (site 2). Despite being out from dawn I saw almost no birds at all; winter and spring are clearly better times to visit.

2. This crossroads (28.1785N, 14.2490W), and the track to the right (signposted to La Pared 1 hr 45) is where several observers have seen bustards and coursers, especially by looking down the slopes towards the sea.

3. The crossroads can also be reached from the Costa Calma-La Pared road (FV-605). Drive up this road from Costa Calma until, just before the brow of the hill, you see a white sign ('Pueblo del Mar') on the hillside to the left. A track to the left (28.2022N, 14.2192W) passes in front of this sign. If you take the next left you are on a track that eventually (after 4 km) reaches 'the crossroads' but it soon becomes rather rough so again, I chickened out of following it all the way. Instead I parked after 900 metres (28.1990N, 14.2270W) and explored the plateau and the seaward slopes. I found nothing of note but Brian Small has described this as a reliable spot for seeing Houbara, at least in spring.

4. An exceptionally good place to see Black-bellied Sandgrouse is at their regular drinking site at La Pared. Follow the FV-605 from Costa Calma until you see a track to the left into La Pared. Take this track then turn right at the first roundabout following signs to Bahia La Pared. This road ends at a car park (28.2179N, 14.2191W) and cafe with a barranco to your left. Up to 100 sandgrouse come to drink in the barranco each morning at around 10pm but are best viewed from 100 metres back along the road. Stay in your vehicle to avoid disturbance; even then you may find they only perch on the opposite slope and are reluctant to come to the water in which case you should move away. The barranco also has Fuerteventura Chat and Spectacled Warbler as well as the inevitable Berthelot's Pipit, Great Grey Shrike and Raven.

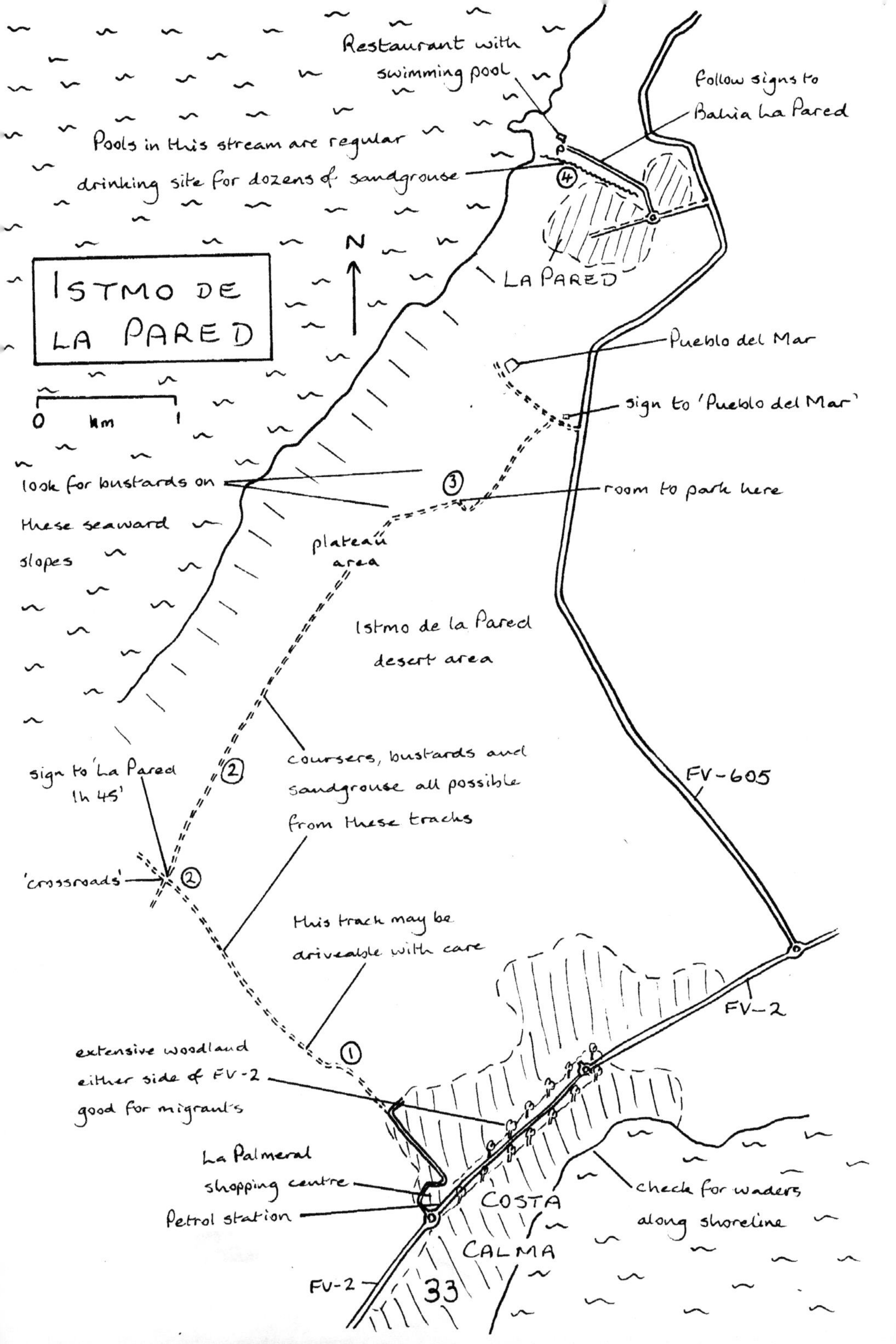

Restaurant with swimming pool
follow signs to Bahia La Pared
Pools in this stream are regular drinking site for dozens of sandgrouse
4
LA PARED
N
ISTMO DE LA PARED
0 km 1
Pueblo del Mar
sign to 'Pueblo del Mar'
look for bustards on these seaward slopes
3
room to park here
plateau area
Istmo de la Pared desert area
coursers, bustards and sandgrouse all possible from these tracks
FV-605
sign to 'La Pared 1h 45'
2
'crossroads'
2
This track may be driveable with care
FV-2
1
extensive woodland either side of FV-2 good for migrants
La Palmeral shopping centre
Petrol station
COSTA CALMA
check for waders along shoreline
FV-2

Southern Lanzarote

Attraction

Many birdwatchers stay at the resort of Playa Blanca which is expanding out over good birding habitat but desert species such as Houbara and courser can still be found here. The resort is also close to a good seawatching spot and one of the best wetland sites in the Canaries, the Salinas de Janubio.

Getting there

Playa Blanca is about 34 km south of the airport on the LZ-2 or it can be reached by ferry from Correlejo on Fuerteventura.

Notes

1. The well-established hotel gardens around the resort can be good for migrants such as warblers (including Subalpine and Bonelli's) and Flycatchers.

2. Both Houbara Bustard and Cream-coloured Courser have regularly been seen on the stony plain near the cement works. To get there, follow the road out of Playa Blanca towards Papaguayo until you pass the cement works on your left. By turning left at the next roundabout (28.8769N, 13.8130W) you can follow a track through suitable habitat. Scan on both sides of the track.

3. Towards the western end of the resort, the lighthouse at Punta Pechiguera (28.8557N, 13.8724W) makes a good spot to look for passing seabirds though it's possible you'll see nothing more than Cory's Shearwaters.

4. The road past the lighthouse makes a loop to the north. Even as recently as 2013, Houbaras have been seen from here too, on both sides of this road (28.8747N, 13.8706W), although continued development may soon mean you have to scan or walk north from this road to be successful. Your best bet is to find the track (28.8779N, 13.8680W) to the abandoned hotel as this takes you through an expanse of relatively undisturbed habitat (sometimes going by the name 'El Rubicon').

5. The saltpans at Salinas de Janubio are still active but it is the lagoon and associated pools that seem to be better for birds. The map shows several places from which to view the area but the best bet is to drive to the beach at the southern end and check the areas you can reach from there (28.9307N, 13.8281W). As well as being good for a variety of waders, this is a regular site for wintering Black-necked Grebe. Other birds seen here have included Lesser Yellowlegs, Red-necked Phalarope and Roseate Tern. However, in August 2013 there were few birds here - the best was a Ruddy Shelduck.

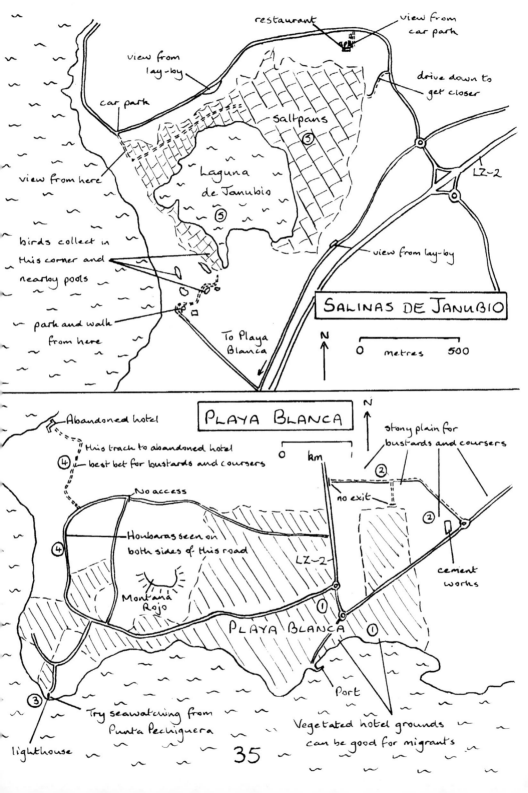

The Teguise Plain

Attraction

Probably the best place in the world to see Houbara Bustard. Few observers fail to see them here; some see 10 or more birds in one visit. There's a good chance of Cream-coloured Courser plus plenty of Stone Curlew (race insularum), Lesser Short-toed Lark and Trumpeter Finch and the chance of Eleonora's Falcon too.

Getting there

The best areas are north of the LZ-30 road between San Bartholome and Teguise and west of the LZ-402 road between Teguise and La Caleta

Notes

1. The first spot to try is found by taking the road from Teguise towards La Caleta and turning left on the first track you see (29.0496N, 13.5843W), after about 500 metres. As you do so you'll see a relatively bushy area in front of you, mostly to the left of the track. Drive slowly past these bushes with frequent stops to scan for Houbaras.

2. There's a chance of Houbaras almost anywhere along the tracks shown on the map so just keep driving, stopping and scanning. Another productive spot is found by turning right at the next crossroads and checking an area with pockets of cultivation. Bustards are often attracted to the insects that feed in these cultivated areas (eg 29.0486N, 13.6032W).

3. If you follow the track from site 2, keeping straight on at the crossroads marked by 3 crosses, but left at the next junction, you can follow this track all the way to Munique. En route the area becomes more open but you pass a number of 'hollows' which should all be checked for Houbaras. To access this same track from Munique, look for a lane (29.0695N, 13.6349W) to the east of the village that begins more or less opposite a house with two stone eagles on the roof.

4. Another track begins (29.0822N, 13.6303W) about 700 metres north of Munique, taking you through much more open desert areas. In 2013, Graham Hogan had 4 Houbaras from this track including one on the left only 300 metres from the road. Just beyond here the stony/sandy plain on the left is particularly good for coursers and the next little patch of cultivation is great for Stone Curlew and Lesser Short-toed Larks which, on my visit, were being chased by an Eleonora's Falcon.

5. Another good bet for Houbara is found by taking the track towards Tao from the LZ-30 San Bartholome-Teguise road. The turning (29.0372N, 13.5945W) is opposite the eastern end of the Prolasa factory area, also called 'Quesaria del Faro'. There's a chance of bustards anywhere along this track but I recommend scanning from near the white hut (29.0382N, 13.6074W) as this spot overlooks plenty of good scrubby areas.

6. There are other tracks into this area from the road to La Caleta. The track opposite the 1 km marker (29.0548N, 13.5847W) and another track 200 metres further on were both partly covered by sand in 2013 so you may prefer to avoid them and reach the same areas via site 3.

7. Continuing towards La Caleta, just past the 2 km marker is a very wide track to the left (29.0653N, 13.5850W) which eventually reaches the village of Soo. Some reckon this is the best track of all for the desert birds. After 2 km it is crossed by a broad hollow with lots of bushes - another potential spot for bustards.

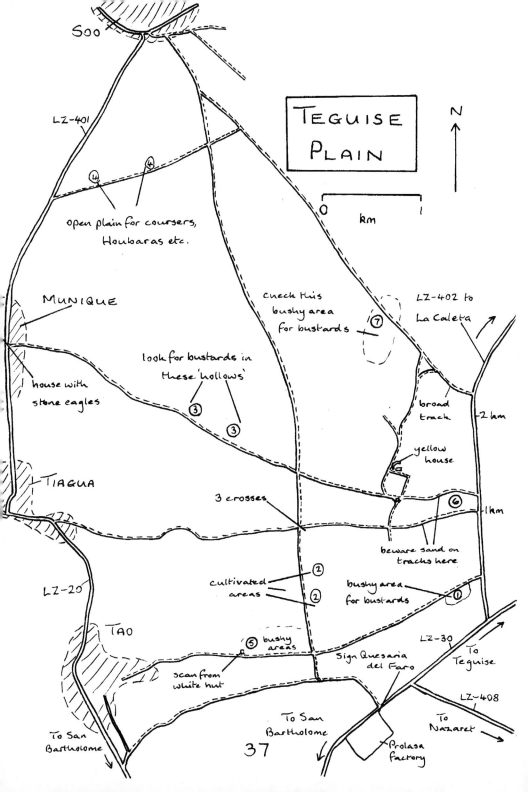

Northern Lanzarote

Attraction

Apart from the desert birds of the Teguise Plain (page 36), the northern part of the island also has sites for Eleonora's Falcon, Barbary Falcon, Canary and Slender-billed Barn Owl. Red-billed Tropicbirds are regularly seen near Orzola and pelagic trips from there give you an almost guaranteed chance of Bulwer's, Madeiran, White-faced and Wilson's Petrels.

Getting there

These areas can be reached from the LZ-1 north from Arrecife or the LZ-10 through Haria.

Notes

1. A total of about 400 pairs of Eleonora's Falcon breeds on the islands off the northern end of Lanzarote (200 pairs on Graciosa, 180 pairs on Roque del Este in 2013). This seems remarkable given the relatively low numbers of passerines that migrate so far out at sea and it means that some of the falcons come looking for birds on the mainland of Lanzarote. One of the best places to look for them is by the small reservoir, the Presa de Mala, just inland from Mala. They are attracted here not so much for food but for a chance to drink and bathe in the reservoir. To get there, turn off the LZ-1 to approach Mala from the north, then turn right at the first proper crossroads (29.0998N, 13.4697W) after 1km. This takes you back over the LZ-1 for about 2 km until you see a track to the reservoir on the right at the second hairpin bend (29.1080N, 13.4800W).

2. Any migrants that get past the offshore gauntlet of Eleonora's Falcons are likely to aim for the greenest parts of the island. The areas in and around the tourist hotels are lusher than most but one of the best spots is the Golf Course at Costa Teguise. To get there yourself, find the LZ-34 road between Costa Teguise and Tahiche and turn off where you see the Club de Golf sign (29.0075N, 13.5225W).

3. The best area of the island for Canaries is around Haria. They can sometimes be found around the village itself or from one of the miradors above the town eg the Mirador de Haria. A short walk with a chance of Canaries begins on the left (29.1327N, 13.5156W) just before the last hairpin as you descend to Haria.

4. There is an area of saltpans at Los Cocoteros, clearly signposted from Guatiza. As you approach Los Cocoteros, the road bends left into the village; at this point carry straight on and take the next track to the left (29.0601N, 13.4674W) to view the saltpans from the south. Collins and Clarke described these as the best site for waders on the island but in August 2013 the small area of pools was dry and there were no waders at all.

5. The north-west coast of Lanzarote is comprised of 10 km of steep cliffs, the Riscos de Famara. There are 8 pairs of Barbary Falcons breeding here. The easiest way to see them is to visit the Mirador del Rio (29.2142N, 13.4810W) a well-known and well-signposted landmark. An entrance fee of 4.5 Euros gets you into a cafe (designed by local art-hero Cesar Manrique) built into the cliff with spectacular picture windows and a verandah. Look right from the verandah to the cliffs below the communications tower and you are likely to spot a distant falcon. Keep scanning and you might get one flying right overhead; Eleonora's Falcons often hunt here too. To avoid paying the entrance fee you could scan the cliffs from one of the approach roads to the mirador or visit another mirador further south by following signs to Guinate Tropical Park. This alternative mirador (29.1847N, 13.5012W) is beyond the entrance to the zoo; the cliff face with white splash marks is closer than at the Mirador del Rio so you may get better views of the falcons here.

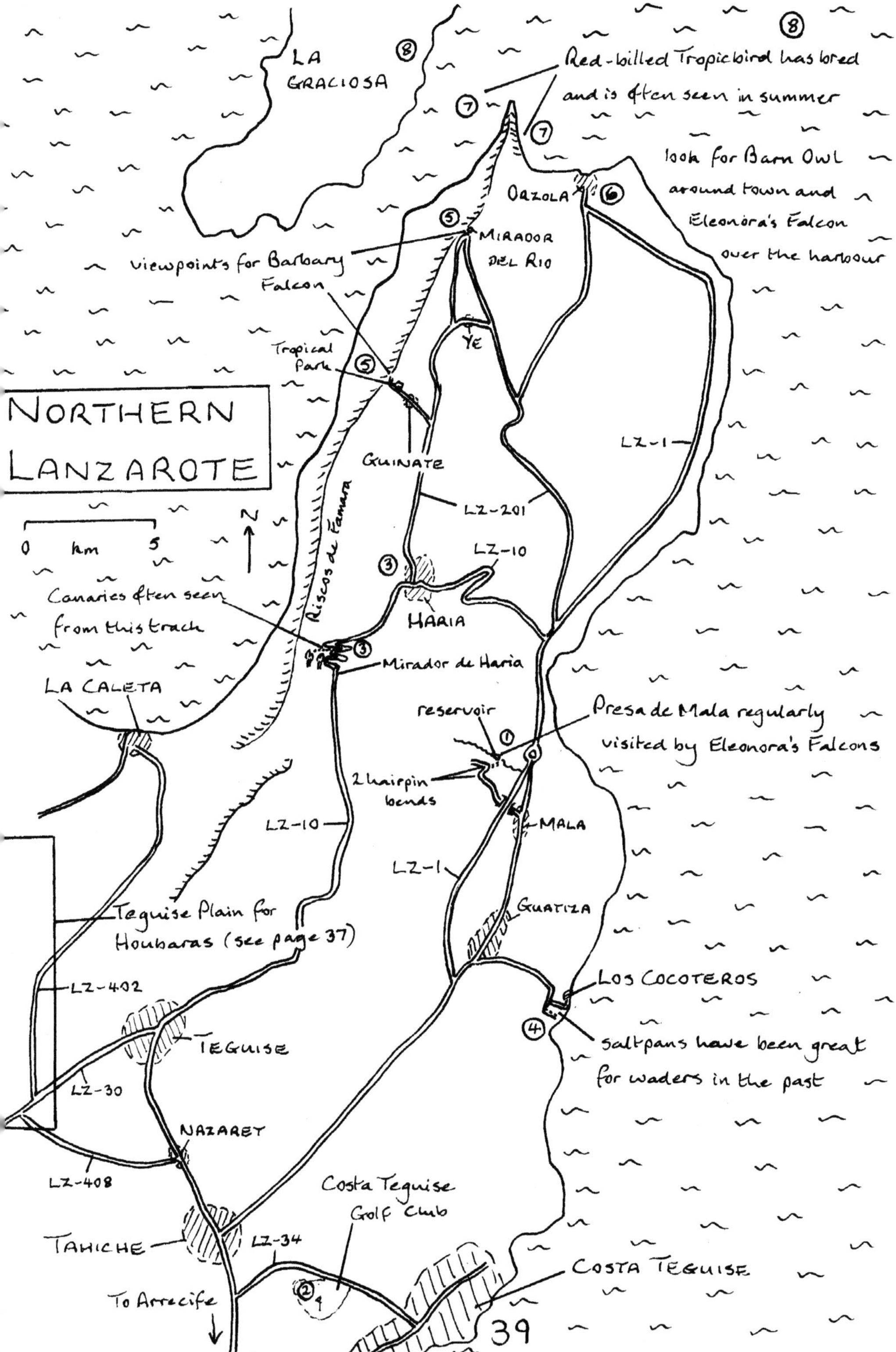

NORTHERN LANZAROTE
LA GRACIOSA
8
8
Red-billed Tropicbird has bred and is often seen in summer
7
7
look for Barn Owl around town and Eleonora's Falcon over the harbour
ORZOLA
6
5
MIRADOR DEL RIO
viewpoints for Barbary Falcon
YE
Tropical Park
5
GUINATE
LZ-1
LZ-201
0 km 5
N
Riscos de Famara
LZ-10
3
Canaries often seen from this track
HARIA
3
Mirador de Haria
LA CALETA
reservoir
1
Presa de Mala regularly visited by Eleonora's Falcons
2 hairpin bends
MALA
LZ-10
LZ-1
GUATIZA
Teguise Plain for Houbaras (see page 37)
LOS COCOTEROS
LZ-402
4
saltpans have been great for waders in the past
TEGUISE
LZ-30
NAZARET
LZ-408
Costa Teguise Golf Club
TAHICHE
LZ-34
2
COSTA TEGUISE
To Arrecife

6. The Barn Owls of Fuerteventura and Lanzarote are of a different race *Tyto alba gracilirostris* which has been proposed as a separate species, the Slender-billed Barn Owl. It nests on sea-cliffs so its breeding sites are difficult to access but hunting birds are regularly seen or heard around the village of Orzola. One option is to eat at the excellent seafood restaurant ('Bahia de Orzola') on the left as you enter the village and hope the owl makes an appearance or calls while you eat. Another strategy is to wait at dusk at the car park (29.2218N, 13.4544W) at the edge of the village looking out for a hunting bird from there. Orzola is also a good place to look for Eleonora's Falcon, with several birds at a time sometimes visible over the harbour

7. For the last couple of summers, up to 5 Red-billed Tropicbirds at once have been seen near Orzola and in 2013 a pair actually bred on the nearby cliffs. In the early part of the breeding season the adults were regularly around the nesting area but once the chick was well-grown they made only infrequent visits. One way to see these birds is to take the ferry from Orzola to La Graciosa and hope you spot one *en route*. Or you can find out whether lanzarotepelagics.com are organising any trips into the bay in a Zodiac which can linger near the nest so that good views are obtained. In 2013 the tropicbirds were seen up to 24th August but on my visit 3 days later they failed to appear.

8. The small islands north of Lanzarote are exceptional for breeding seabirds. the most recent count I can find (2001/02) gives the following numbers of breeding pairs: **Alegranza** - Cory's Shearwater (10,000!), British Storm-petrel (200-300), Bulwer's Petrel (150-200), 'Madeiran' Petrel (50-100), White-faced Petrel (10-15) and Little Shearwater (possibly 10); **Montana Clara** - Cory's Shearwater (1,000), British Storm-petrel (100), Bulwer's Petrel (100-130), 'Madeiran' Petrel (50-70), White-faced Petrel (30-40) and Little Shearwater (20-50); La Graciosa - Cory's Shearwater (300), British Storm-petrel (10-20), Bulwer's Petrel (possibly 5) and possibly 'Madeiran' Petrel and White-faced Petrel too; **Roque del Este and Roque del Oueste** both have small numbers of Cory's Shearwater, British Storm-petrel and 'Madeiran' Storm-petrel though Roque del Oueste also has a few pairs of Bulwer's Petrel.

However, access to the islands is, of course, limited and the birds can be difficult to find at sea even if you get close to the islands on a boat. The best chance of seeing them is to take a pelagic trip to the best feeding area around the Canaries, the Banco de la Concepcion, about 60 km north of Lanzarote. These trips are run by lanzarotepelagics.com who have plenty of experience of finding the birds using well-organised 'chumming' methods. On their trips in August and September you can almost guarantee seeing White-faced, Band-rumped (='Madeiran'), Wilson's, Bulwer's and British Storm-petrel. Our trip in late August also yielded Sabine's Gull, Manx and Great Shearwater, Long-tailed Skua, Grey Phalarope and a Fea's/Zino's Petrel. Earlier in the season you would probably see more White-faced Petrels (they've had up to 300) and later would give you a better chance of finding a South Polar Skua (they've had up to 3). Other birds seen from their boats have included Black-bellied Storm Petrel (twice) and Scopoli's Shearwater. The Band-rumped Petrel complex, formerly known as Madeiran Petrel, seems likely to consist of 4 species in the eastern North Atlantic, one breeding in summer in the Canaries, another breeding in winter in the Canaries and others breeding in the Azores and the Cape Verde islands. Photographic evidence suggests they have been seeing 3 of these different types (all except 'Cape Verde' Storm-petrel).